Who Was Abraham Lincoln?

ABRAHAM LINCOLN

Who Was Abraham Lincoln?

by Janet B. Pascal

illustrated by John O'Brien

Penguin Workshop

For David and Susan,
who are pretty good with their axes, too—JBP

PENGUIN WORKSHOP
An Imprint of Penguin Random House LLC, New York

Text copyright © 2008 by Janet B. Pascal. Illustrations copyright © 2008 by John O'Brien. Cover illustration copyright © 2008 by Penguin Random House LLC. All rights reserved. Published by Penguin Workshop, an imprint of Penguin Random House LLC, New York. PENGUIN and PENGUIN WORKSHOP are trademarks of Penguin Books Ltd. WHO HQ & Design is a registered trademark of Penguin Random House LLC. Printed in the USA.

Visit us online at www.penguinrandomhouse.com.

Library of Congress Control Number: 2008010694

ISBN 9780448448862   45 44 43

Contents

Who Was
Abraham Lincoln?

April 11, 1865. After four terrible years, the American Civil War—the war between the North and the South—was almost over. Now it was clear that the North would win. President Abraham Lincoln had fought the war to prevent the rebel South from leaving the Union. He wanted the country to stay *one* country—the United States of America.

From the window of the White House, the president addressed the big crowd below. His twelve-year-old son, Tad, was at his feet, collecting the pages of the speech as the president dropped them to the floor.

A man in the audience called out, "What shall we do with the rebels?"

Someone answered, "Hang them!"

Before the president could answer, Tad piped up. "No, we must hang *on* to them."

Sometimes Tad understood his father better than anyone else. President Lincoln wanted to hang on to the defeated Southern states. He wanted to make them feel that once again they were part of the Union. He wasn't interested in revenge. Lincoln was a remarkable president and a remarkable man. He hoped to turn his enemies back into his friends.

Chapter 1
Life in a Log Cabin

The man who is often called America's greatest president was born on February 12, 1809, in a crude log cabin in Kentucky. Eighteen feet long and sixteen feet wide, it had a dirt floor and no windows.

LOG CABIN

CABIN INTERIOR
ONE ROOM PLUS A LOFT

His father, Thomas Lincoln, was hardworking and quiet, and famous for his honesty. He'd had little schooling—just enough to sign his name. Abraham's mother, Nancy Hanks Lincoln, was intelligent and curious. She could read a little, but couldn't write at all.

The Lincolns were poor. They moved from one small farm to another, trying to scratch out a living. When Abraham was seven, the family moved from Kentucky to Indiana.

One reason for the move was that Kentucky was a "slave state," while Indiana was a "free state." The Lincoln family hated slavery. Abraham later said that he was "naturally antislavery" as far back as he could remember. Eventually, the Lincolns ended up on a tiny farm in Illinois.

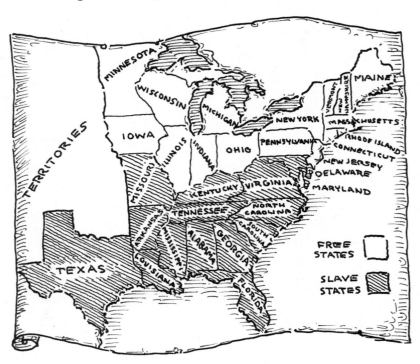

Even as small children, Abraham and his older sister, Sarah, worked hard. Abraham was tall and strong for his age. By the time he was eight, he could pick up an ax and split wood as well as any man. He also helped with the plowing and harvesting. But not hunting—when he was seven years old, he shot a wild turkey and discovered that he hated killing things.

When Abraham was nine, his mother

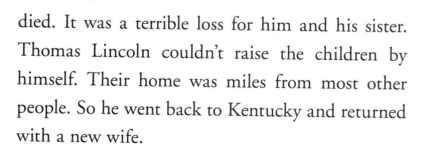

died. It was a terrible loss for him and his sister. Thomas Lincoln couldn't raise the children by himself. Their home was miles from most other people. So he went back to Kentucky and returned with a new wife.

Sarah Bush Johnston was a widow with three children. She brought her furniture with her—real beds, a table, and chairs that seemed like amazing luxuries to the Lincoln children. Much as he missed his own mother, Abraham quickly came to love Sarah. She encouraged all his interests. He called her "Mama" and was much closer to her

than to his own father. Because of Sarah, Abraham remembered his childhood as a happy time.

With so much work to do, there wasn't much time for schooling. Anyway, out in the wilderness there weren't many schools. In Kentucky, Abraham had gone to an "A, B, C school," where he had learned the alphabet, but not how to read or

write. In Indiana, he sometimes went to a "blab school"—a place where all the students said their lessons out loud together. The schoolmaster listened and tried to pick out their mistakes through the noise.

Abraham finished with school for good at the age of fifteen. Altogether, he had gone for only about a year. But he had learned how to read. Now he could teach himself anything he wanted. He read every book he could find. He once walked twenty miles to borrow one.

It took him a long time to finish a book. Many

LINCOLN'S BOOKS

MOST OF THE BOOKS ABRAHAM LINCOLN READ AS A CHILD WERE ONES HIS STEPMOTHER, SARAH, BROUGHT WITH HER WHEN SHE MARRIED HIS FATHER. THERE WAS THE BIBLE, OF COURSE, AND ALSO AESOP'S FABLES. HE LOVED THESE FABLES, WHICH TAUGHT HIM HOW TO USE FUNNY LITTLE STORIES TO MAKE IMPORTANT POINTS. HE MEMORIZED PASSAGES FROM SHAKESPEARE, AND COULD STILL RECITE THEM WHEN HE WAS PRESIDENT. ANOTHER FAVORITE BOOK WAS A BIOGRAPHY OF GEORGE WASHINGTON. AS A CHILD, THOUGH, LINCOLN COULDN'T HAVE KNOWN THAT SOMEDAY HE WOULD BE CONSIDERED JUST AS GREAT A PRESIDENT!

people thought he seemed slow and plodding. But his stepmother understood why he took so long to learn. He wanted to be sure he really understood everything. Sometimes he'd learn part of a book by heart. Because paper was expensive and hard to get, he wrote out passages on a piece of wood. When the wood got so black he couldn't see what he was writing, he would shave it off. Then he would start over again.

People liked Abraham. He was so good at telling funny stories. He was also famous for practical jokes. He once managed to have two men who were getting married on the same day delivered to the wrong brides. People were still talking about this joke years later.

Chapter 2
The Wider World

Abraham Lincoln knew he didn't want to be a farmer like his father. But he didn't know what he did want to do. So when he was twenty-one, he decided to leave home and find out.

He was hired to help sail flatboats loaded with supplies down the Sangamon River. One time, the boat got stuck on a dam in front of the town of New Salem in central Illinois. It began filling with water. Lincoln and the others onboard couldn't free it. Suddenly Lincoln had a brilliant idea. He bored a hole in the front of the boat and shifted all the supplies to that end. The boat tipped toward the hole and all the water ran out until the boat was high enough to go over the dam. Denton Offutt, the boat's owner, was so impressed that he offered to put Lincoln in business. He decided to build a store in New Salem. Lincoln would manage it.

NEW SALEM

New Salem was a small village. But to Lincoln it seemed large and bustling. The store was a place

where people gathered. Lincoln quickly became popular. People trusted him. He would never take advantage of anyone, even for a few cents. He joined a debating club and took part in town politics. He also went to the meetings of the local court. The justice of the peace began asking his opinion on cases, because what he said was always so funny. But his opinions were also very intelligent. Soon people began coming to Lincoln for legal advice.

Lincoln didn't just impress people in town. Some rough farm boys called the Clary's Grove gang had heard about Lincoln—the young man everyone was praising so much. They wanted to take him down a peg. So they challenged him to a wrestling match. We don't know whether Lincoln won or lost. But the way he took on the whole gang won the boys over. They became his friends and loyal supporters, too.

In 1832, Lincoln's friends convinced him to run for the Illinois State Legislature. He didn't win, but he came close. In the meantime, Offutt's store failed, and Lincoln lost his job. Just then, a war broke out between the Illinois settlers and Native Americans. Lincoln joined the militia. He never actually fought any battles. But he boasted about all the blood he'd shed—because of the mosquitoes.

He decided to run for the state legislature again. He could count on support from all his friends in New Salem. But some farmers thought he was just a town fellow who didn't know how to work in the fields. So Lincoln pitched in with the harvest.

That won him the farmers' votes. And he could count on the Clary's Grove gang to make sure their friends would vote for him, too. This time, Lincoln won.

Lincoln decided he would be a better representative if he knew more about law. So he began to read law books. Although he never studied law formally, Lincoln taught himself enough to earn his law license by studying every spare second of the day. Often he studied while lying on his back, with his long legs resting on the trunk of a tree. As the sun moved, he followed it around the tree.

LINCOLN'S DEPRESSION

LINCOLN ENJOYED LIFE. HE WAS USUALLY IN THE CENTER OF A CROWD, TELLING STORIES. WHEN HE REACHED THE PUNCH LINE, NO ONE LAUGHED HARDER THAN HE DID. BUT EVERYONE AROUND HIM NOTICED THAT HE ALSO CARRIED WITH HIM A TERRIBLE SADNESS. SOMETIMES, ONLY AN HOUR AFTER HE HAD BEEN TELLING JOKES, HE MIGHT BE FOUND SITTING ALONE, HUNCHED UP WITH HIS ARMS AROUND HIS KNEES. NO ONE DARED TO GO NEAR HIM DURING THESE TIMES. LINCOLN SUFFERED FROM ATTACKS OF DEPRESSION ALL HIS LIFE.

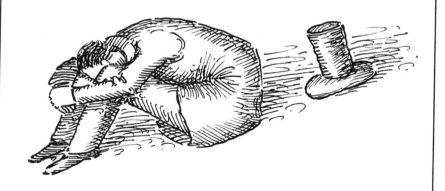

Chapter 3
A Member of Congress

In 1837, Lincoln moved to Springfield, the new state capital. Springfield was still a frontier town with log cabins. Pigs ran loose on the dirt roads. But it was the biggest place Lincoln had ever lived in. It even had a bookstore. He worked at a friend's law firm, where he kept track of the paperwork. He wasn't very good at this. He had a habit of carrying important papers around inside his tall stovepipe hat. Sometimes he lost them.

The state government was only in session for part of the year. And there wasn't enough business in Springfield for a lawyer to live on. So like most Western lawyers, Lincoln had to travel to towns all around the state. Twice a year, a judge visited all the towns that were too small to have their own courts. Lincoln joined the group of lawyers who followed the judge's route.

Everyone traveled together. At night they all crowded into small rough inns. Sometimes twenty men had to squeeze into one room. Lincoln often slept on the floor. After a few days, the group

would move on. Sometimes the roads were so bad, they had to walk. Because Lincoln had such long legs, his companions made him wade across streams first to find out how deep they were.

WHIGS AND DEMOCRATS

THE UNITED STATES HAS HAD MANY DIFFERENT POLITICAL PARTIES IN ITS HISTORY, OFTEN WITH CONFUSINGLY SIMILAR NAMES. (THERE WAS EVEN A PARTY CALLED THE DEMOCRATIC-REPUBLICANS.) WHEN LINCOLN WAS STARTING OUT, THE MAIN PARTIES WERE THE WHIGS AND THE DEMOCRATS. THE DEMOCRATS SUPPORTED STATES' RIGHTS. THEY THOUGHT EACH STATE SHOULD HAVE THE POWER TO RULE ITSELF.

THE WHIGS WANTED A STRONGER CENTRAL GOVERNMENT. THEY SAID THE GOVERNMENT SHOULD ENCOURAGE AND PAY FOR IMPROVEMENTS THAT WOULD MAKE THE COUNTRY WORK BETTER. LINCOLN WAS A WHIG. IN HIS EARLY CAREER HE SUPPORTED THE BUILDING OF CANALS AND RAILROADS THAT WOULD HELP MAKE TRADE AND TRANSPORTATION EASIER.

Lincoln didn't mind the bad food or the rough life. He liked meeting people. He impressed them with his funny stories, his friendliness, his skill, and his honesty. "If . . . you cannot be an honest lawyer," he said, "resolve to be honest without being a lawyer."

Lincoln was a strong supporter of the Whig Party. Soon he became one of the most important party members in Illinois. Wherever he went, he worked hard campaigning for Whig candidates. He knew thousands of voters by name.

Lincoln was comfortable with most people, but he was shy and awkward around young women. A couple of years after he moved to Springfield, he met Mary Todd at a party. Although he stepped all over her feet when they danced together, Mary liked Lincoln. She was a Southern belle who, at twenty-one, was very eager to get married. Pretty and lively, she put Lincoln at ease by doing most of the talking herself. Mary was

more interested in politics than most women of the time. She often said that she wanted to marry a man who would be president.

They were married on November 4, 1842. Lincoln joked about how strange it was that anyone would marry him. "Nothing new here," he wrote to a friend, "except my marrying, which to me, is a matter of profound wonder." On Mary's wedding ring, Lincoln engraved "Love is eternal."

At first the couple lived in a hotel, but soon they bought a house. It was tiny and not very fancy. Still, it was the first house Lincoln had ever owned. Nine months after the marriage, their first child, Robert, was born. Two years later they had a second son, Edward, who died at age three. Eventually they had a third son, Willie, and a fourth, Thomas. When Thomas was born, his head was so large that Lincoln thought he looked like a tadpole. So the boy was nick-named Tad.

Both parents spoiled their children. When Lincoln brought the boys into his law office, they dumped ashtrays and inkstands on the floor. They piled up papers and danced on them. Lincoln's

PHOTOGRAPHY

WHEN ABRAHAM LINCOLN WAS BORN, PHOTO-GRAPHY DIDN'T EXIST. DURING HIS LIFETIME, NEW METHODS OF TAKING PERMANENT PICTURES WERE INVENTED. IT BECAME FASHIONABLE TO SIT FOR YOUR PORTRAIT. SO WE KNOW JUST WHAT LINCOLN AND HIS FAMILY LOOKED LIKE. THE EARLIEST KNOWN PHOTOGRAPH OF LINCOLN WAS TAKEN AROUND 1846 (BEFORE HE HAD HIS BEARD). A PHOTOGRAPH OF MARY WAS TAKEN AT THE SAME TIME.

PHOTOGRAPHY ALSO MADE THE CIVIL WAR MORE REAL TO PEOPLE THAN ANY EARLIER WAR. MATHEW BRADY AND HIS ASSISTANTS WENT OUT TO THE BATTLEFIELDS AND RECORDED EXACTLY WHAT THEY SAW. BRADY PHOTOGRAPHED LINCOLN SEVERAL TIMES, AS WELL.

THE LINCOLNS BY 1853

partner said he sometimes "wanted to wring their little necks." But Lincoln never scolded his boys.

In 1841, after six years in the state legislature, Lincoln decided it was time to do something bigger and more important. He wanted to be the Whig candidate for the United States House of Representatives. But the party chose another candidate. Even so, he worked hard to get his rival elected. He thought this might put him in line to be elected the next time.

His plan worked. In 1846, Abraham Lincoln was elected as a representative from Illinois. He moved into a boardinghouse in Washington, D.C. Now Lincoln would be dealing with issues that affected the whole country, not just his own state.

Mary and the children came with him, but the boys behaved so badly that soon he had to send them away. Lincoln didn't have time to miss them. He was working hard. He almost never missed a session of Congress. He served on committees.

He made speeches. But he didn't do anything very important, and no one noticed him. At the end of his two-year term, Lincoln returned home feeling that he had failed to make his mark on the country.

For the next six years, Lincoln concentrated on his law practice back in Springfield. He had decided he wasn't interested in politics.

Chapter 4
The Great Debater

What brought Lincoln back to politics was the Kansas-Nebraska Act of 1854. For a long time, Americans had been arguing about slavery. Should it be legal? And if so, where? In 1820, Missouri had become a state. Slavery was legal there. At that time, Congress had declared that this was as far north as slavery could go. In any land north of the Missouri border, slavery would never be allowed.

Then, in 1854, Congress went back on that decision. The Kansas-Nebraska territory was north of the border limiting slavery. But now Congress said that when the territory became two separate states, the people there could decide about slavery. They could make it legal if they wanted. Had Congress broken its promise? Abolitionists—

people who were fighting to make slavery illegal—
thought so. They hated the Kansas-Nebraska Act.

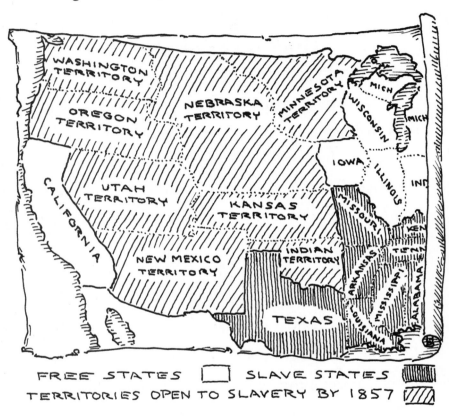

FREE STATES ☐ SLAVE STATES ▥
TERRITORIES OPEN TO SLAVERY BY 1857 ▨

Lincoln did, too, even though he was not exactly
an abolitionist. He hated slavery and wanted it to
end. But he thought the Constitution said slavery

was legal in the United States. He was afraid that if Congress tried to force slave owners to give up their slaves, it would just lead to violence. And so, although slavery went against his own values, he supported the legal rights of slave owners.

Lincoln thought slavery could end another way. He thought slavery should only be allowed in the part of the United States where it was already legal. But it should not be allowed into any new territory. Then it would die out in time. People would come to see that slavery was bad for the country. They would be willing to end it without fighting. To Lincoln, the Kansas-Nebraska Act was a terrible step in the wrong direction. Congress was opening up huge new areas of the country to slavery.

So Lincoln returned to politics. The man responsible for the Kansas-Nebraska Act was Senator Stephen Douglas from Illinois. Lincoln and Douglas had been rivals for years—ever since they were in the state legislature together.

ABOLITIONISTS

MOVEMENTS OPPOSING SLAVERY BEGAN IN AMERICA WHILE THE COLONIES WERE STILL UNDER BRITISH CONTROL. BY 1804, SLAVERY HAD BEEN MADE ILLEGAL IN ALL THE NORTHERN STATES.

IN THE 1830S AND 40S, AN ACTIVE ABOLITIONIST MOVEMENT DEVELOPED IN THE UNITED STATES. ABOLITIONISTS BELIEVED THAT SLAVERY WAS EVIL AND SHOULD BE COMPLETELY ILLEGAL EVERY-WHERE. MANY WROTE ARTICLES AND PRESSURED THE GOVERNMENT FOR REFORM. SOME WERE ACTIVE ON THE UNDERGROUND RAILROAD–THE SECRET NETWORK THAT HELPED SLAVES ESCAPE TO FREEDOM.

NOT EVERYONE WHO WAS AGAINST SLAVERY WAS AN ABOLITIONIST. SOME PEOPLE WERE AFRAID THAT ABOLITIONISTS WERE DANGEROUS. THEY WANTED TO MAKE BIG CHANGES TOO QUICKLY. THE MOST EXTREME ABOLITIONIST WAS JOHN BROWN. HE TRIED TO START AN ARMED SLAVE REBELLION, BUT HE WAS CAPTURED AND HANGED.

STEPHEN DOUGLAS

Douglas had become famous, while Lincoln was still relatively unknown. Now Lincoln was eager to challenge him.

Douglas, however, refused to set up a debate. So Lincoln followed him to an open-air speech in Springfield. Douglas defended the Kansas-Nebraska Act. He said that in America, people had the right to decide how they wanted to be governed. This meant that the people of every state should be able to decide freely whether or not to allow slavery. When Douglas had finished, Lincoln yelled to the crowd that tomorrow he would explain why Douglas was wrong.

The next day, a huge audience gathered. Lincoln spoke for three hours. Douglas's arguments, he

said, only made sense if you didn't think of blacks as people. Lincoln thought blacks should have the same right to decide about their lives as white people. He said that America had been founded on the belief that "no man is good enough to govern another man *without that other's consent,*" no matter what color the person was.

DRED SCOTT DECISION

THE KANSAS-NEBRASKA ACT WAS NOT THE
ONLY THING THAT MADE LINCOLN AFRAID THE
COUNTRY WAS MOVING IN THE WRONG DIRECTION.
IN 1857, THE SUPREME COURT HAD DECIDED ON
THE CASE OF DRED SCOTT. SCOTT WAS A SLAVE
WHOSE MASTER
HAD BROUGHT HIM
TO LIVE IN ILLINOIS
AND IN WISCONSIN
TERRITORY.
SLAVERY WAS
ILLEGAL IN BOTH
PLACES. SCOTT
SAID THIS MEANT
HE WAS NOW FREE.
THE COURT DECIDED
AGAINST HIM. THEY
SAID IF A SLAVE
HAD BEEN BOUGHT
LEGALLY, HE WAS

DRED SCOTT

STILL A SLAVE, NO MATTER WHERE HE WAS. IN
EXPLAINING THEIR DECISION, ONE OF THE JUSTICES
WROTE THAT BLACK PEOPLE "HAD NO RIGHTS
WHICH THE WHITE MAN WAS BOUND TO RESPECT."

Lincoln's speech made him famous. In 1854, he decided to run for Senate. He came very close, but was not elected. In the meantime, the important issues of the day were breaking up the old political parties. There were many issues, but slavery was the one on everyone's mind. Many Democrats had left their party in anger over the Kansas-Nebraska Act. The Whigs, too, were split on the issue of slavery. Lincoln was no longer sure where he fit in.

A new political party was being founded in order to fight slavery. Its members called themselves Republicans. Lincoln had been a loyal Whig all his life. But now he became a leader in the new party. Their first presidential candidate was the explorer and military leader John C. Frémont. Lincoln was almost chosen as the candidate for vice president, but he didn't quite make it. In any case, Frémont lost. James Buchanan, who supported slavery, became president.

Refusing to be discouraged, Lincoln challenged Douglas for his seat in the Senate. The Illinois Republicans nominated him unanimously. His acceptance speech was based on a quotation from the Bible. The phrase became one of his favorites: "A house divided against itself cannot stand." The United States, he said, could not continue as half-free and half-slave. Either slavery would

JAMES BUCHANAN

end, or it would take over the whole country. Or the country would be destroyed.

Chapter 5
Mr. President

Once again Lincoln asked Douglas to debate him. This time, Douglas had to accept. In 1858, seven debates were held in different towns all over Illinois. The main issue was slavery. People poured in from neighboring states to listen. The whole country followed the Lincoln-Douglas debates in the newspapers. Reporters wrote down every word each man said.

Lincoln and Douglas made comical opponents. Douglas was short, round, and dignified. His nickname was "The Little Giant" because he dressed elegantly and had a rich, deep voice. Lincoln was tall, thin, and awkward. He still dressed like a farmer, and had a high, thin voice. Douglas traveled to the debates in a private carriage.

Lincoln rode the train with everyone else, joking and chatting. But both men were very skilled speakers.

People disagreed about who had won the debates. And Lincoln lost the Senate election again. But he had become famous. He was invited to lecture on slavery in New York City. He won over the huge crowd with his passion and simple, logical arguments. This was his first public appearance on the east coast, the center of political power in the United States.

While Lincoln was making a name for himself, the country was moving toward a crisis. States in the South talked about leaving the United States to form their own country. President Buchanan was a weak leader who didn't know how to control the South. He couldn't even keep the support of his own party. In 1860, the Democratic Party could not agree on whom to support for president. They were split between Stephen Douglas and another candidate.

The Republican Party chose Lincoln as their candidate for president. They called him "the rail

LINCOLN'S VIEWS ON BLACK PEOPLE

ALTHOUGH LINCOLN DID NOT THINK BLACKS SHOULD BE SLAVES, HE DID NOT SUPPORT COMPLETE EQUALITY FOR THEM, EITHER. HE DID NOT THINK THE TWO RACES COULD EVER LIVE TOGETHER COMFORTABLY. SO HE SUGGESTED THAT FREED SLAVES SHOULD BE SENT TO A COLONY SOMEWHERE. IT TOOK HIM YEARS TO REALIZE THAT MOST BLACKS DIDN'T WANT TO

MOVE TO A NEW COUNTRY—THEY WANTED RIGHTS
IN THEIR OWN COUNTRY. OF COURSE LINCOLN DIDN'T
ACTUALLY KNOW MANY BLACK PEOPLE. LATER, WHEN
THE CIVIL WAR BROUGHT HIM INTO CONTACT WITH
THEM, HE BECAME MORE OPEN-MINDED. THE NEW
YEAR'S DAY PARTY THE LINCOLNS GAVE IN 1864
WAS THE FIRST EVENT EVER AT WHICH BLACKS
WERE GUESTS AT THE WHITE HOUSE.

candidate" because he had split rails as a boy. The name told people that he was an ordinary, hard-working man just like them. He did very little campaigning. He didn't really expect to win. On the night of the election, Lincoln and his fellow Republicans crowded into the state capitol. News about the election kept coming in by telegraph. At two A.M. the result was certain. Because the Democratic Party was divided between two candidates, Lincoln had won more votes than any other candidate. Mary was thrilled—she had always wanted to be the wife of a president. But Lincoln could not sleep. "I then felt as I never had before the responsibility that was upon me," he said.

He was an unlikely president. He'd had only one year of school. He had almost no experience in national government. He was not a war hero. He'd spent his whole life in pioneer towns. He'd been defeated every time he ran for the Senate. He didn't even know exactly what a president did. And now, suddenly, he was the sixteenth president of the United States.

GAZETTE

"A HOUSE DIVIDED AGAINST ITSELF CANNOT STAND."

LINCOLN

During the campaign, an eleven-year-old girl named Grace Bedell had written to him. She said she thought he'd look more like

a president if he had a beard. So now he grew one.

Chapter 6
Civil War

Lincoln was in trouble before he even took office. The slave states hated him. Almost no one in the South had voted for him. As soon as the news came of his election, seven states seceded from the Union. They said they were no longer part

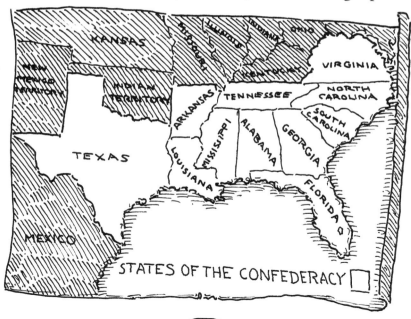

STATES OF THE CONFEDERACY ☐

JEFFERSON DAVIS

of the United States. Lincoln was not their president. Soon, four more states joined them. They called their new country the Confederate States of America. They elected Jefferson Davis as their president.

In his brief inauguration speech, Lincoln spoke to a huge crowd gathered in front of the capitol. He told them he would not let the nation become two countries, no matter what. He avoided talking about slavery. He had a good reason for this. Four states where slavery was legal—Delaware, Maryland, Kentucky, and Missouri—had not left the Union. Lincoln didn't want to anger these states and lose them, too.

But despite Lincoln's wishes, the country was soon torn in two. A month later, on April 12, 1861, Southern soldiers fired on Union soldiers at Fort Sumter in South Carolina. The Civil War had begun.

FORT SUMTER

FREDERICK DOUGLASS

FREDERICK DOUGLASS WAS A SLAVE WHO ESCAPED AS A YOUNG MAN. HE BECAME AN INSPIRING LECTURER AND AUTHOR. DOUGLASS BELIEVED IN FREEDOM AND EQUALITY FOR ALL PEOPLE, INCLUDING WOMEN. HE DID NOT ALWAYS SUPPORT LINCOLN. HE BELIEVED LINCOLN WAS MUCH TOO CAUTIOUS ABOUT ENDING SLAVERY. AFTER THE EMANCIPATION PROCLAMATION, WHICH FREED THE SLAVES IN THE REBELLING SOUTHERN STATES, DOUGLASS BEGAN TO THINK BETTER OF THE PRESIDENT. ONCE THEY MET, HE WAS

COMPLETELY WON OVER. DOUGLASS SAID LINCOLN TREATED HIM EXACTLY AS HE WOULD HAVE TREATED ANY MAN, DESPITE THE DIFFERENCE IN THEIR SKIN COLOR.

More than eighty years earlier, the American colonies, north and south, had united to break away from England and become a new country. Now Americans would be fighting Americans. Families were divided—even Lincoln's own family. His wife, Mary, had relatives in the South who owned slaves. They fought on the other side.

UNION
SOLDIER :
BLUE

CONFEDERATE
SOLDIER :
GRAY

Lincoln had no trouble getting volunteers for the army. People in the North supported the war, and everyone thought it would be over soon. Lincoln believed that to fight a war, the president needed more power than in peacetime. There are some things the president is not supposed to do without the approval of Congress. Lincoln went ahead and did them, anyway—he built up the army and spent money on weapons. He also limited freedoms that were set down in the Constitution. He said that people who threatened the war effort could be sent to prison without a trial. They didn't even have to be told what their crime was. Because the war was so popular, Congress let Lincoln get away with it.

The war did not end quickly. On both sides, soldiers died in bloody battles that didn't accomplish anything. Lincoln's army didn't seem to have a plan for winning the war. People began to wonder if Lincoln was up to the job. The president is the commander in chief of the army, but Lincoln had never fought in any battles. He needed to teach himself about winning a war. Until he did, he would have to rely on his generals to advise him. And, unfortunately, some of his generals weren't very good.

Lincoln needed an army. What he had was a bunch of eager, inexperienced volunteers. He chose General George B. McClellan to turn them into real soldiers.

GENERAL GEORGE B. McCLELLAN

In some ways, McClellan was a very smart choice. He was organized and good at details. The soldiers trusted him to take care of them. Unfortunately, he wasn't very good at actually fighting battles. He was too cautious. He kept refusing to attack the Confederate army. He was afraid his army wasn't ready. He was afraid the Confederate army was too strong. He lost chances to win battles that could have ended the war. Finally Lincoln became impatient. "If General McClellan does not want to use the army," he said, "I would like to *borrow* it for a time."

While Lincoln was learning to be a president, his family was settling into their new home. The White House was much fancier than any place

THE WHITE HOUSE

they had lived before, but it was dirty and run-down. Congress gave Mary some money to fix it up. She made it elegant and beautiful. However, she spent far too much money. Lincoln rarely lost his temper with his wife. Now he did. He needed money from Congress to pay for uniforms and blankets for soldiers. Yet he had to go and ask for more money for silly frills, as well. It had to stop, he told his wife.

Lincoln's oldest
son was away at
college. But
ten-year-old
Willie and
eight-year-
old Tad had a
wonderful time
in Washington.

They made friends with soldiers
who were quartered in the White House. They
set up toy cannons on the roof and fired at the
Confederate army only a few miles away.

It was unusual for children to be living in the White House. The presidents before Lincoln had only grown-up children. The whole country was interested in the Lincoln boys. People sent them presents, especially pets. They had a pony and two goats that ran around and destroyed the White House gardens. Sometimes the goats got inside the house. Tad once made a sled out of a chair and had a goat pull him right through the middle of an elegant party.

Lincoln never scolded the boys or tried to make them behave. Neither did Mary. They were allowed to burst into the president's office—it didn't matter

who was there. Lincoln sometimes talked to his generals with one of the boys climbing up his chair and onto his shoulders. Sometimes they napped on the floor, overhearing state secrets.

The boys had a soldier doll named Jack. One day they decided that Jack had gone to sleep on guard duty and had to be punished. They sentenced him to death. Then they ran to their father, interrupting a meeting, and asked him to pardon Jack. Lincoln listened gravely to their case. Then he wrote out an official pardon on White House stationery.

Later, Tad also got Lincoln to free a turkey that was being fattened for Christmas dinner. Tad wanted to keep it as a pet. (He named the turkey Jack, too.) Lincoln didn't mind these interruptions. In fact, he needed them. In the middle of this terrible war and with all his worries, Tad and Willie could make him smile.

His sons weren't the only people interrupting Lincoln. Almost anyone who waited long enough outside his office was invited in. Most came to ask for favors. For example, they hoped Lincoln would find a government job for them. Sometimes

there were such huge crowds that the staircase was completely blocked.

The most painful requests were from parents and wives begging Lincoln to pardon a soldier. Perhaps their son had been condemned to death for cowardice or neglecting his duties. Lincoln always tried to grant these requests. He understood that

sometimes a man meant to be brave but just had "cowardly legs" that made him run away from battle. Lincoln's openness to ordinary people earned him their loyalty, even when the war seemed endless. They called him "Father Abraham."

Lincoln's sympathy with other parents was strengthened by his own loss. In 1862,

eleven-year-old Willie Lincoln died of typhoid fever. His death was terribly hard on both parents. Of all their sons, Willie had been most like his father. Mary fell apart after Willie's death. She couldn't believe he was really gone. She began to hold séances, hoping the spirits of both her dead sons—little Eddie and Willie—would visit her.

A lot of people in Washington had never liked

Mary. They thought she showed off. People whispered mean rumors. Some even said she was a Confederate spy. After all, she had brothers and sisters who sided with the South. The rumors were completely unfair. Mary may have been vain and irritating, but she was always loyal to her husband and to the Union. Anyone who was Lincoln's enemy was her enemy, too—even her own brother. But she was so unpopular that some people actually said maybe Willie's death wasn't all bad. It might stop Mary from making a fool of herself in public.

Lincoln was as brokenhearted over Willie's death as Mary. Sometimes he hid in his room so he could weep in peace. But after the first day, he never broke down in public.

Chapter 7
The End of Slavery

As the war neared the end of its second year, more than one hundred battles had been fought, with many thousands of men wounded and killed. And still, neither side was winning. In the North, it became harder and harder to find men who were willing to join the army. And the government was running out of money to pay for the war.

The South had broken away to keep slavery. Yet, so far, Lincoln had avoided dealing with slavery directly. Now he realized he had to face the issue. Abolitionists supported the war because they thought it would end slavery. They wanted Lincoln to make it illegal once and for all. But even in the North, a lot of people were against this idea. Lincoln was afraid to lose their support. So he hesitated.

He wasn't sure that the president had the power to outlaw slavery. He had sworn to protect the laws of the United States, and slavery in the South was legal. The president couldn't just overturn laws all by himself. That had to come from the people. Only the citizens of the country could change the United States Constitution.

At last, Lincoln came upon a way to do what he thought was right and at the same time obey the Constitution. A country at war was allowed to seize property that the enemy was using to fight the war. Southern states were using slave labor in many ways that helped the war effort. Lincoln decided this was a good legal reason to take slaves away from their owners in the rebel states.

Congress began to pass laws that chipped away at slavery. Slaves who escaped from rebel owners or were captured by the Union army would not be returned to their owners. They were free.

Then Lincoln decided to go further. Quietly, all by himself, he wrote the Emancipation Proclamation. This proclamation did *not* free all slaves. It was an act of war, and it applied only to Confederate states. In the rebel states, all slaves would be freed forever. But in Delaware, Maryland, Kentucky, and Missouri, slavery remained legal because these states had stayed with the Union.

Lincoln was sure that, once the nation was reunited, it would be possible to end slavery in the whole country. But that had to be done by Congress. As president, he only had power to act against states that were rebelling.

Of course there was no way to enforce the Emancipation Proclamation until the Union had won the war. Just because the proclamation told Southerners to free their slaves, it didn't mean they would. Lincoln knew this. He said he felt like someone trying to make a law to change the behavior of a comet. But now he had made it clear that the Union planned to end slavery for good. When Lincoln talked to his cabinet, he told them he was not asking their advice. He had made up his mind.

The act took effect on January 1, 1863. Slaves in the South heard the news. Right away, many of them escaped and went north. The Union army

began to form regiments of black soldiers. As free men, they would now fight against their former masters. By the end of the war, almost 200,000 blacks had joined the Union army.

Chapter 8
A Two-Minute Speech

Finally, Lincoln found a brilliant general to lead his army: Ulysses S. Grant. Grant was willing to fight. He had already won important victories, such as the Battle of Vicksburg, which gave the Union control of the Mississippi River. But Grant realized that just winning battles was not enough to win the war. The important thing was to take away the South's ability to keep on fighting. To do this, the Union army had to attack in many places at once.

They had to fight battles one right after another. And they needed to destroy railroads and factories that helped keep the Confederate army going. Grant planned to wear out the South so it would have to surrender. But it would take time. And it would cause many thousands more deaths.

Lincoln relied on Grant more and more. After one terribly bloody battle, many people thought  Grant should be fired. But "I can't spare this man," Lincoln said. "He fights."

In the North, fewer men were willing to volunteer as soldiers. So in 1863, Lincoln called for a draft. For the first time in American history, men were forced to enlist in the army. In New York and other cities,

there were draft riots. Men said they didn't see why they should die to free black people. Many Northerners were so fed up with the war, they were even willing to just let the rebel states go.

More and more, people blamed Lincoln. He needed to explain why the war had to be fought to the bitter end. But back then the president didn't often address the nation directly. Lincoln's chance came at the dedication of the cemetery in Gettysburg, Pennsylvania. The Battle of Gettysburg had been a great victory for the

GETTYSBURG NATIONAL CEMETERY

Union. Union soldiers had stopped the rebels from pushing their way north. But more than three thousand Union soldiers and almost five thousand Confederate soldiers had been killed, and a special cemetery was created to bury them all.

The dedication of the cemetery took place on November 19, 1863. Even though Lincoln was the president, he was not the main speaker. That was Edward Everett, a man famous for long, fancy speeches. Everett talked for almost two hours. Lincoln spoke for only two minutes. His words were simple and direct. He began by quoting a line from the Declaration of Independence: "All men are created equal." He reminded his audience that the United States was the first country founded on that idea of equality. In 1776, no one had known if such a country could work. Now people were wondering if it could last. Maybe it was about to fall apart. Lincoln could not give in to the rebels' demands, because the country had to survive.

The Union was fighting to keep the United States united, but also to guarantee that "government of the people, by the people, for the people, shall not perish from the earth."

According to some listeners, the end of Lincoln's speech was greeted with silence. People were too moved even to clap. Edward Everett wrote that Lincoln, in two minutes, had gotten to the heart of the subject better than his own entire long speech. History agrees with Everett. The Gettysburg Address is widely considered one of the most beautiful and important speeches ever written.

But the war had gone on for almost a thousand days, and there was still no end in sight.

THANKSGIVING

EVER SINCE THE PILGRIMS, AMERICANS HAVE CELEBRATED DAYS OF THANKSGIVING. BUT UNTIL 1863 THERE WAS NO ONE DAY OF THE YEAR THAT PEOPLE THOUGHT OF AS THANKSGIVING DAY. SARAH JOSEPHA HALE (WHO WROTE THE NURSERY RHYME "MARY HAD A LITTLE LAMB") THOUGHT THERE SHOULD BE. STARTING IN 1827, SHE WROTE TO EVERY PRESIDENT, URGING HIM TO ESTABLISH ONE. BUT NO ONE LISTENED UNTIL ABRAHAM LINCOLN. AFTER THE VICTORY AT GETTYSBURG, HE ISSUED A PROCLAMATION SETTING ASIDE THE LAST THURSDAY OF NOVEMBER AS A DAY TO GIVE THANKS FOR THE SURVIVAL OF THE NATION.

Chapter 9
The War Is Won

In 1864, Lincoln's first term as president was coming to an end. There was supposed to be an election in November. But was it possible to hold an election during a civil war? Lincoln's advisers suggested putting it off until the war was over. He refused. "We cannot have free government without elections," he explained. So a campaign began, although people in the rebel states would not be voting. Lincoln's opponent was George McClellan, the general who wouldn't fight. In his speeches, McClellan hinted that he would be willing to compromise to end the war.

Lincoln was not at all sure he would win the election. Many Americans were fed up with the war. They were ready to vote for anyone who

promised a quick end. But Lincoln knew that the soldiers supported him. So he made sure they were able to vote.

Then, right before the election, the Union won some huge victories. General William Sherman, who had been trained by Grant, captured Atlanta. General Philip Sheridan, also trained by Grant, won a series of battles in the Shenandoah Valley. And Grant himself was close to taking the Confederate capital at Richmond, Virginia. With faith in the

war restored, the voters elected Lincoln to a second term.

By the beginning of 1865, the end of the war was finally in sight. On March 25, Grant's army captured Richmond. Then he cornered the troops of General Robert E. Lee, the leader of the Confederate army. Lee had no choice. On April 9, he surrendered his army to Grant at Appomattox, Virginia. For all practical purposes, the Civil War was over.

Lincoln was not present for the surrender. The two generals met in a courthouse. Grant was careful to treat Lee generously. He knew that was what Lincoln wanted. The defeated soldiers would not be paraded through the streets or mocked. They would even be allowed to keep their horses. And Grant arranged for food to be given to the starving Confederate troops.

Back in Washington, excited crowds surrounded the White House. Everyone was calling for Lincoln. Tad was given a big cheer when he appeared at the window waving a Confederate flag. Then Lincoln arrived. He asked the band to play the Southern song, "Dixie." He had always liked the tune, he said, and now the

song belonged to the whole country again.

Lincoln had been planning for this day for a long time. Bringing back peace was even more important than waging war. And it was going to be just as difficult. With Lincoln's encouragement, Congress passed the Thirteenth Amendment to the Constitution. This amendment would outlaw slavery everywhere in the United States.

In his second inaugural speech, Lincoln had said that he wanted to welcome the rebel states back to the Union. But as he spoke to the crowd outside the capitol building, not everyone was cheering for him. A photograph shows John Wilkes Booth and his comrades standing nearby. These men were already plotting to kill the president.

JOHN WILKES BOOTH

Booth was a successful actor. Some people called him the handsomest man in America. He was devoted to the Confederacy and believed slavery was not just good for white people—it was even good for black people. He despised Lincoln, who he thought was rude and uncultured. He was sure Lincoln was destroying the country.

About a month into his second term, Lincoln

RECONSTRUCTION

LINCOLN WANTED TO WELCOME THE REBEL STATES BACK TO THE UNION WITH OPEN ARMS. AFTER LINCOLN'S DEATH, HIS VICE PRESIDENT, ANDREW JOHNSON, TRIED TO FOLLOW LINCOLN'S WISHES. BUT HE DID NOT BELIEVE IN EQUAL RIGHTS FOR BLACKS. EVEN SO, CONGRESS PASSED THE FOURTEENTH AND FIFTEENTH AMENDMENTS, GRANTING BLACKS CIVIL RIGHTS AND GIVING BLACK MEN THE RIGHT TO VOTE. THE SOUTH HAD TO BE FORCED TO ACCEPT THEM. TO DO THIS, INSTEAD OF RESTORING THE REBEL STATES TO THEIR FULL

ANDREW JOHNSON

RIGHTS, AS LINCOLN HAD HOPED TO DO, CONGRESS IMPOSED A MILITARY GOVERNMENT ON THEM. IT WAS THE BEGINNING OF YEARS OF VIOLENCE AND RACIAL HOSTILITY. WOULD LINCOLN HAVE DONE A BETTER JOB? WE WILL NEVER KNOW.

had a terrible dream. In it, he walked into the White House and saw himself lying dead in a coffin. He asked a guard what had happened. The guard said, "He was killed by an assassin."

Three days later, on April 14, 1865, Lincoln went to a comedy at Ford's Theatre with his wife and some friends. He and Mary wanted to relax and enjoy themselves. That afternoon he had said to her, "We must *both* be more cheerful in the future." At the theater, Lincoln sat in a rocking

chair and Mary hung on his arm and flirted with her husband.

John Wilkes Booth learned Lincoln was going to be at the theater. Booth had acted there and knew his way around the building. So he had no trouble getting in and sneaking upstairs to the president's private box. He crept up behind

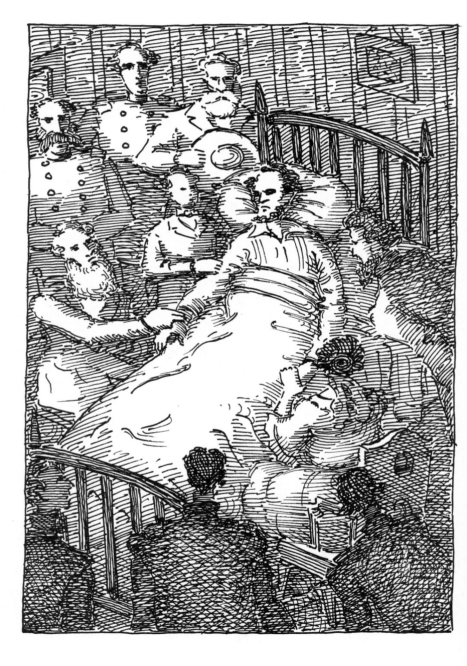

Lincoln and fired his gun. The sound of Booth's gunshot was drowned out by laughter from the audience. Booth escaped by leaping dramatically to the stage. This was a showy move he had often used when he was acting.

Lincoln did not die immediately. He was carried from the theater to a house across the street. The bed there was so small that the tall president didn't fit on it. He had to be propped up on pillows. Surrounded by his family, doctors, and advisers, he lay in a coma for nine hours. At 7:22 the next morning, Abraham Lincoln died. He was fifty-six years old.

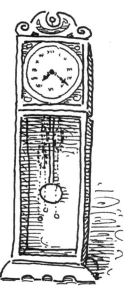

Chapter 10
Farewell to the President

John Wilkes Booth was never brought to trial. A few days after the shooting, his hiding place was discovered. He was shot to death trying to escape.

Booth thought what he'd done was noble and heroic. However, all over the nation, people mourned the dead president. Clocks were stopped to mark the moment of his death. Millions came to Washington, D.C., to pay their respects. Then Lincoln's body was put on a special train back to Springfield. That was where he would be buried. His son Willie's coffin was dug up and traveled

with him. The train retraced the route Lincoln had taken when he first came to Washington as president. At each stop, there were elaborate parades with the coffin mounted on a wagon. Sometimes the lines were three miles long. People waited hours for the chance to say good-bye to the president they had loved.

Mary Lincoln never really recovered from the shock of her husband's death. She was too upset to go to the funeral. Even now, people criticized her. They said when she left the White House she took things that didn't belong to her. Her later life was not happy.

Tad's death—probably from tuberculosis—at age eighteen was a terrible blow. Of all her children, only Robert lived to be an adult. But he and Mary did not get along. For a while he had her locked up in a hospital, claiming that she was insane. Robert had a long career as a lawyer and diplomat. He had three children and several grandchildren. Robert lived to be eighty-two, dying in 1926.

Today, two hundred years after his birth, Abraham Lincoln is more honored than any other president except perhaps George Washington. He appears on the penny and the five-dollar bill.

He has a monument in the nation's capital.

LINCOLN MEMORIAL

His face is carved on Mount Rushmore. Many cities, several mountains, five national parks, and nineteen counties have been named after him. Hundreds of books have been written about him. He is remembered along with Washington on Presidents' Day.

MOUNT RUSHMORE

Almost from the moment of his death, Lincoln became a larger-than-life figure. People saw him as a kind of saint. Of course he was just a man. He made mistakes and he held some opinions that are hard to accept today. But it is clear he was no ordinary man. He kept the country together during one of its darkest times. America was lucky to have him.

LINCOLN MEMORIAL

ONLY TWO YEARS AFTER PRESIDENT LINCOLN'S DEATH, CONGRESS FIRST RAISED THE IDEA OF BUILDING A MONUMENT TO HONOR HIM. THE LINCOLN MEMORIAL WASN'T FINISHED UNTIL 1922, HOWEVER. LINCOLN'S SON ROBERT WAS STILL ALIVE AND WENT TO THE DEDICATION CEREMONY. THE MEMORIAL IS MODELED ON A GREEK TEMPLE, WITH A HUGE STATUE OF LINCOLN INSIDE. (ON THE BACK OF A PENNY, IF YOU LOOK AT THE PICTURE OF THE LINCOLN MEMORIAL, YOU CAN SEE A TINY STATUE BETWEEN THE MIDDLE COLUMNS.) ON THE WALLS OF THE TEMPLE ARE ENGRAVED THE GETTYSBURG ADDRESS AND HIS SECOND INAUGURAL SPEECH. BUT THE ENGRAVER ACCIDENTALLY CARVED "EUTURE" INTO THE STONE, INSTEAD OF "FUTURE." YOU CAN STILL SEE WHERE THE MISSPELLING HAD TO BE FIXED.

SEVERAL IMPORTANT EVENTS IN BLACK HISTORY TOOK PLACE AT THE LINCOLN MEMORIAL. IN 1963, MARTIN LUTHER KING DELIVERED HIS FAMOUS "I HAVE A DREAM" SPEECH FROM THE STEPS OF THE MONUMENT.

THE GETTYSBURG ADDRESS

Fourscore and seven years ago our fathers brought forth on this continent a new nation, conceived in liberty and dedicated to the proposition that all men are created equal. Now we are engaged in a great civil war, testing whether that nation or any nation so conceived and so dedicated can long endure. We are met on a great battlefield of that war. We have come to dedicate a portion of that field as a final resting-place for those who here gave their lives that that nation might live. It is altogether fitting and proper that we should do this. But in a larger sense, we cannot dedicate, we cannot consecrate, we cannot hallow this ground. The brave men, living and dead who struggled here have consecrated it far above our poor power to add or detract. The world will little note nor long remember what we say here, but it can never forget what they did here. It is for us the living rather to be dedicated here to the unfinished work which they who fought here have thus far so nobly advanced. It is rather for us to be here dedicated to the great task remaining before us—that from these honored dead we take increased devotion to that cause for which they gave the last full measure of devotion—that we here highly resolve that these dead shall not have died in vain, that this nation under God shall have a new birth of freedom, and that government of the people, by the people, for the people shall not perish from the earth.

TIMELINE OF ABRAHAM LINCOLN'S LIFE

1809 —— Abraham Lincoln is born February 12

1818 —— Nancy Hanks, his mother, dies

1819 —— Lincoln's father marries Sarah Bush Johnston

1831 —— Lincoln moves to New Salem, Illinois

1834 —— Elected to the Illinois General Assembly

1836 —— Receives his law license

1842 —— Marries Mary Todd in Springfield, Illinois

1846 —— Elected to the U.S. House of Representatives

1856 —— Helps organize the new Republican Party

1858 —— Debates Stephen Douglas

1860 —— Elected sixteenth president of the United States;
Southern states begin to secede from the Union

1861 —— Civil War begins

1862 —— Lincoln issues the Emancipation Proclamation

1863 —— Lincoln delivers the Gettysburg Address

1864 —— Lincoln is reelected president

1865 —— General Robert E. Lee surrenders, ending the Civil War;
John Wilkes Booth shoots and kills Lincoln

TIMELINE OF
THE WORLD

Edgar Allan Poe and Charles Darwin are born — **1809**

War of 1812 between — **1812**
United States and Great Britain begins

Francis Scott Key writes "The Star-Spangled Banner" — **1814**

The Missouri Compromise establishes — **1820**
slave-free territory in the United States

Saxophone invented — **1841**

Revolutionary wars are fought in — **1848**
countries all over Europe

First telegraph sent by transatlantic cable — **1858**

Charles Darwin publishes *On the Origin of Species* — **1859**

Florence Nightingale founds a school for nurses in England — **1860**

Serfs are freed in Russia — **1861**

Congress authorizes the building of — **1862**
a transcontinental railroad

The first African-American regiments — **1863**
in the United States Army are formed

The Thirteenth Amendment to the United States — **1865**
Constitution ends slavery in the United States

BIBLIOGRAPHY

Donald, David Herbert. **Lincoln.** New York: Simon & Schuster, 1995.

Freedman, Russell. **Lincoln: A Photobiography.** New York: Clarion Books, 1987.

Pinkney, Andrea Davis. **Abraham Lincoln: Letters from a Slave Girl.** New York: Winslow Press, 2001.

Stone, Tanya Lee. **Abraham Lincoln: A Photographic Story of a Life.** New York: DK Children, 2005.

Rabin, Staton, illustrated by Bagram Ibatoulline. **Mr. Lincoln's Boys.** New York: Viking Children's Books, 2008.

YOUR HEADQUARTERS FOR HISTORY

Activities, Mad Libs, and sidesplitting jokes!
Discover the Who HQ books beyond the biographies

Who? What? Where?

Learn more at whohq.com!